Kids Can Be Awar

Creative lessons for teaching kids about ecology

Written by Rhoda Orszag Vestuto and Doris Larsen

Illustrated by April Hartmann

Teaching & Learning Company

1204 Buchanan St., P.O. Box 10
Carthage, IL 62321-0010

This book belongs to

_____

Cover art by April Hartmann

Copyright © 2003, Teaching & Learning Company

ISBN No. 1-57310-386-1

Printing No. 987654321

Teaching & Learning Company
1204 Buchanan St., P.O. Box 10
Carthage, IL 62321-0010

At the time of publication, every effort was made to insure the accuracy of the information included in this book. However, we cannot guarantee that the agencies and organizations mentioned will continue to operate or to maintain these current locations.

Table of Contents

Dear Teacher or Parent,

Kids Can Be Aware was written for the teacher, parent educator, caregiver or any parent who is looking for a unique curriculum to teach children ecological and environmental concepts.

Kids Can Be Aware is innovative and easy to use:
- It contains fun activities appropriate for preschoolers, kindergartners and special education students.
- It includes all necessary patterns, samples and recipes.
- It uses theme-related experiences and hands-on activities.
- It is consistent with current scientific knowledge and simplifies the concepts for children.
- It enables children to connect the present to the future.
- It sensitizes children to the world around them and helps to develop responsibility towards other people, animals and the environment.
- It affords many opportunities to practice ecology.

Sincerely,

Rhoda   Doris

Rhoda Orszag Vestuto & Doris Larsen

Setting the Scene
The Environment

Discussion

Tell the children that when you look up at the night sky you see planets, stars and empty space. We are looking at all these things from our planet—the Earth. The Earth is our home in space. It provides us with all we need to live and grow. Discuss some of the essential things that we do need to live and grow, such as heat and light from the sun, water, air, etc. More than likely the children will mention cities, cars, toys, houses and other man-made places and objects. Acknowledge that man has made many changes on the Earth. (Section 3, "Pictures of the Future," deals with this issue in depth.) However, before man, the Earth itself was changing very slowly over time and it continues to do so. Discuss what the Earth was like long ago compared to today. Talk about prehistoric animals, habitats, climate, etc. Use the key words below to guide the discussion.

Key Words

• **environment:** The world around us including the sun, water, air, habitats, etc.

• **habitats:** Places where plants and animals have all they need to live. A habitat can be as small as a twig or as large as: 1) A *rain forest* which is a thick forest often found in hot, damp places around the middle of the Earth (the equator). 2) A *desert* which is usually hot, dry and sandy with few plants and little water. 3) An *ocean* which is a huge body of water. 4) A *prairie* which is mostly covered by grasses and has good soil for growing crops. 5) A *swamp* which is a wetland or marsh where the ground is wet and spongy. 6) A *mountain* which is a part of the Earth that reaches hundreds of feet into the air, often capped with snow.

• **climate:** The usual pattern of weather over many years (i.e., cold climate at the poles; hot, wet climate at the equator and milder conditions in between).

Crafts

• Mountain Habitat, page 8.

• Tropical Rain Forest Habitat, pages 9-17.

Enrichment/Language Activities

Science Lab/Study Center

• This center should be set up, built upon and maintained throughout all studies and activities in this book.

Suggested Materials

2 small, leafy plants in pots
small paper bag
1 stalk celery
food coloring
glass jar
candle
jar with cover
large jar with cover
ice
1 plastic sandwich bag for each child
spaghnum moss (air plant)
magnifying glass
box of sand
small cactus
small rocks or pebbles

Resource Materials

• Magazines such as *National Geographic, Ranger Rick* and *Smithsonian.* Books from the library on habitats.

Suggested Activities & Experiments for Children

1. Children make habitat collages. (See "Mail," page 21.)

2. To demonstrate that plants absorb water, fill a glass with water, add food coloring and place a celery stalk in the glass. Watch the celery drink water.

3. To demonstrate the importance of water to life, make a hydroponic garden. (See "Mail," page 23.)

4. To demonstrate the water cycle on Earth, fill a large jar half full with ice cubes and cover it. Children will observe drops of water forming on the outside of the jar. Explain that, as the ice melts and the water becomes warmer, it changes to a vapor or gas. As the vapor cools, it changes back to a liquid.

5. To demonstrate the importance of the sun to life, cover one plant completely with the paper bag or place plant in a dark closet and allow second plant to be exposed to the sunlight. Observe the differences in the plants in one or two weeks.

6. To demonstrate the existence of air, light a candle in a jar and then cover. Observe what happens to the flame as oxygen is used up.

7. Children collect seeds in plastic bags (apple, orange, bean, popcorn, etc.). Seeds may be planted and studied.

8. Children examine spaghnum moss, other plants, leaves and collected seeds with a magnifying glass.

9. Children make and care for a "desert habitat." Place a small cacti in a box of sand along with some small rocks or pebbles.

10. Study pictures of various habitats using resource books.

Booklet

• Worksheets are presented in each of the three sections of this book. Make a cover to keep them in using wallpaper that is either textured or printed with flowers, ferns, etc. See pages 18-20 for specific "Setting the Scene" worksheets.

Mail Call

Suggested Materials

paper	envelopes
small bags	boxes
cards	tape
string	rubber bands
stickers or other types of stamps	

Preparation

• Set up a classroom "mailbox" and pick a day of the week to be Mail Day. Each week appoint a student to be the mail carrier. The mail may be either individual letters, cards, packages or one letter, card or package for the class. Address as you would any letter or package. See pages 21-23 for specific "Setting the Scene" mail.

Snack Time

• See page 24 for recipes.

Setting the Scene
The Environment

Mountain Habitat

Bulletin Board

Suggested Materials: white, blue, brown and green butcher paper; polyester stuffing or batting; newspapers; blue, green and yellow construction paper; variety of colored tissue, crepe or construction paper for flowers, trees and bushes; textured wallpaper samples or sandpaper; scissors; shades of green paint; glue; stapler

Children do as much of the following as their ability allows:

Directions

1. Cover the top half of the bulletin board with blue butcher paper.

2. Cut out meadows and hills from green butcher paper and staple to the bulletin board.

3. Draw three mountains on brown butcher paper and cut them out. Dip fingers in shades of green paint and walk fingertips on the mountains to create vegetation.

4. Cut out and glue snow on the top section of the mountains. Staple on the bulletin board and stuff the mountains with newspapers to give them a 3-D effect.

5. Cut out and staple the following to the scene: blue river, sun, rocks from sandpaper and clouds from batting or polyester.

6. Cut out tree trunks from textured wallpaper or sandpaper. Cut out treetops from green paper. Staple the trees on the scene.

7. Make flowers, grasses and bushes from various colors of tissue, crepe or construction paper. Staple to the bulletin board.

Animals, houses, etc., will be added later.

The Environment

Tropical Rain Forest Habitat

Jungle

Children do as much of the habitat as their ability allows:

Directions

1. Make vines, flowers, ferns, banana stalk and leaves. See pages 10-17.

2. Pick an area of the room for the Tropical Rain Forest Habitat. Hang vines with flowers attached from the ceiling or over the light fixtures. Hang ferns and banana leaves with a stalk of bananas from the ceiling or attach to a wall, door or bulletin board.

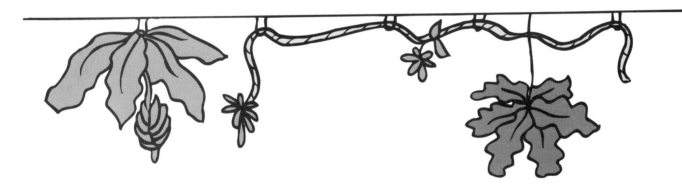

Vines

Suggested Materials: brown tissue paper
(may substitute rope, braided twine or any other material similar to the vines)

Directions

Tightly twist the brown tissue paper, overlap the ends and continue to twist until reaching the desired length.

The Environment

Tropical Rain Forest Habitat

Fern Leaf

Suggested Materials: green construction paper;
one green, 12"-long pipe cleaner for each leaf; stapler; scissors

Directions

1. Fold a piece of 12" x 12" green construction paper in half. Trace the pattern and cut out.

2. Open the leaf and place 2$\frac{1}{2}$"-3" of the pipe cleaner on the base of the leaf for a stem.

3. Refold the leaf and staple the stem in place. Reopen.

4. Connect several leaves by twisting the stems together to make a plant.

Place on fold.

Tropical Rain Forest Habitat

12-Petal Flower

Suggested Materials: brightly colored construction paper; scissors; glue

Directions

1. Fold an 8$\frac{1}{2}$" square of construction paper in half twice to form a 4$\frac{1}{4}$" square. Cut out the pattern, lay the pattern on the fold, trace and cut out the petals.

2. Repeat step 1 using 5" x 5" paper and 3" x 3" paper.

3. Open and then crease the petals as shown to give dimension for the flower.

4. Put a drop of glue in the center of the largest petals and place the next size in the center. Repeat for the smallest petals.

5. Attach to vines, ferns, etc.

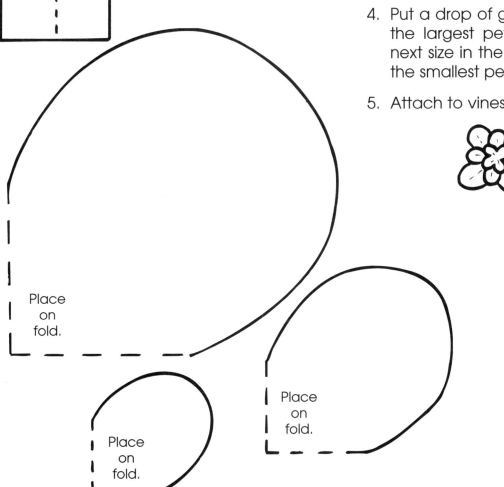

Place on fold.

Place on fold.

Place on fold.

Tropical Rain Forest Habitat

Bromeliad (Air Plant)

Suggested Materials: green, brown and a variety of brightly colored tissue paper; scissors; tape

Directions

1. Cut 7" x 20" strip of green tissue paper.

2. Cut in spikes to within 2¹/₂"-3" of the bottom of the strip.

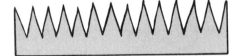

3. Cut a 6" x 20" strip of brightly colored tissue paper and cut in spikes as above.

4. Roll brightly colored tissue paper into a cylinder and secure with tape.

5. On the outside of the brightly colored cylinder, roll a green tissue strip.

6. Carefully pull up the center of the brightly colored tissue to form a flower.

7. Gently bend the green spikes downward to form leaves.

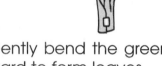

8. Wrap the remaining base around the vine and secure with tape.

9. Tightly twist the 12" length of green or brown tissue paper to form the roots and drape between the flower and the vine.

Tropical Rain Forest Habitat

Orchid

Suggested Materials: a variety of brightly colored tissue paper including green; tape; green construction or butcher paper; scissors

Directions

1. Fold 7" x 7" square of brightly colored tissue paper in half twice to make a 3^1/$_2$" square.

2. Place the petal pattern from page 14 on the fold, trace and cut out.

3. Cut a 3" x 6" strip of brightly colored tissue paper for the orchid center.

4. Roll the strip into a cylinder and secure with tape.

5. Shape the top by cutting. Cut four tabs in the bottom.

6. Place the orchid center in the middle of the petals and tape the tabs to the petals.

7. Tightly twist the green tissue paper for the stem and roots.

8. Using the pattern on page 14, cut out leaves of green 8^1/$_2$" x 3" construction paper.

9. Glue or tape the flower to the stem, the stem to the vine and the leaves to the base of the stem. Drape the roots between the flower and the vine.

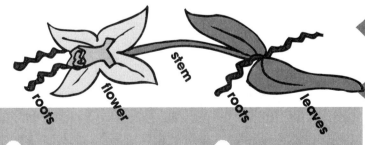

roots flower stem roots leaves

Tropical Rain Forest Habitat

Orchid Petal and Leaf Patterns

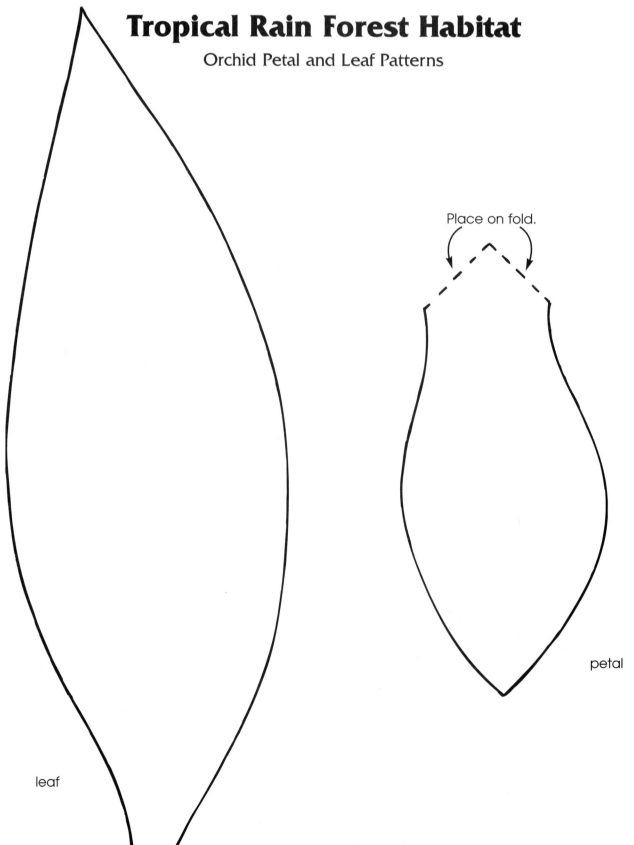

Place on fold.

petal

leaf

Tropical Rain Forest Habitat

Banana Stalk Base

Suggested Materials: manila or yellow construction paper or poster board, scissors

Directions

1. Fold a 9" x 18" paper in half.

2. Trace the pattern and cut out.

3. Add the stem, flower and fruit from page 17.

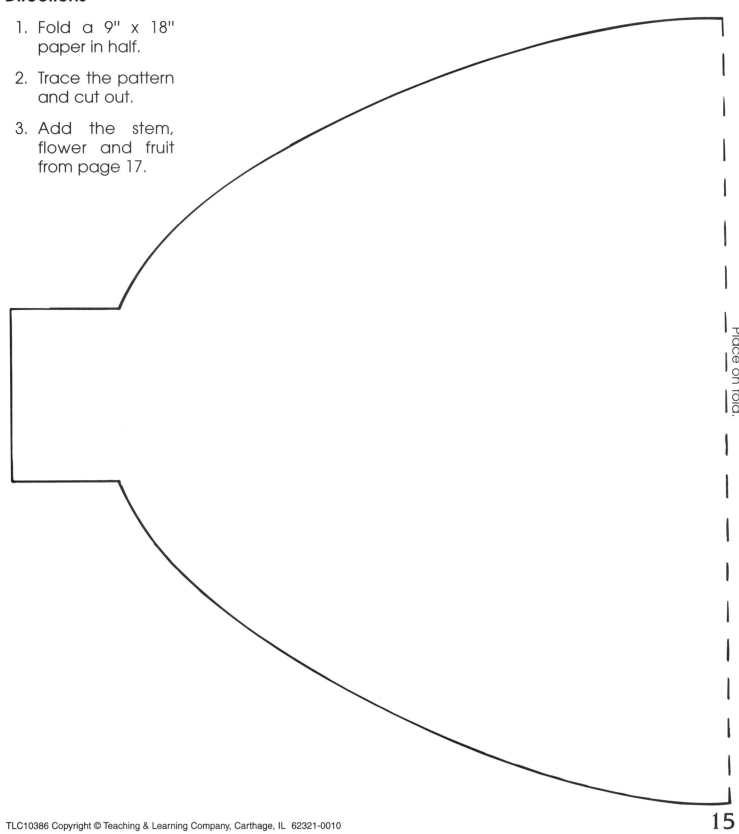

Place on fold.

Tropical Rain Forest Habitat

Banana Leaf

Suggested Materials: 12" x 18" green construction paper or finger paint paper and green finger paint, 12"-long green pipe cleaner for each leaf, scissors, stapler

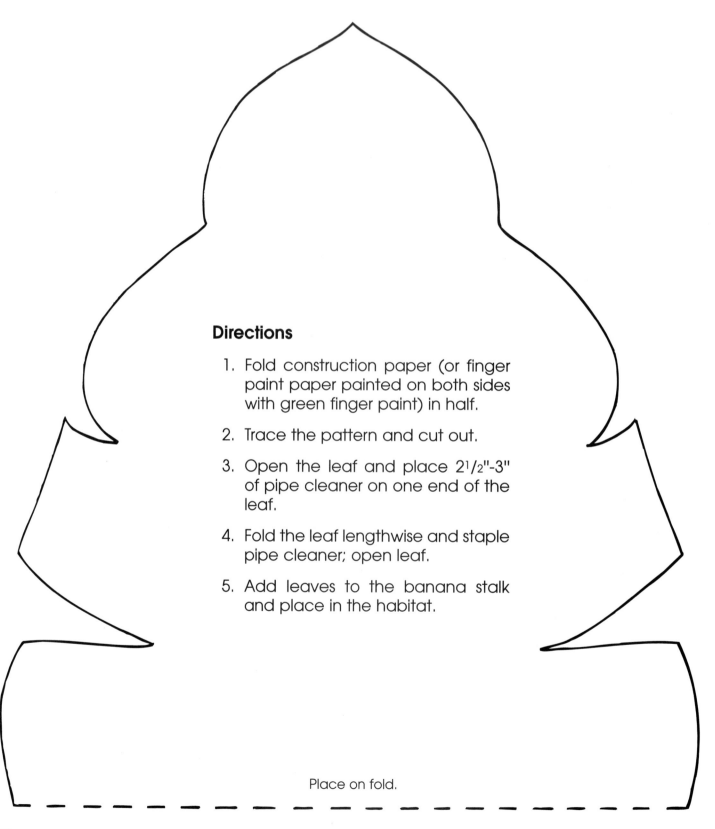

Directions

1. Fold construction paper (or finger paint paper painted on both sides with green finger paint) in half.

2. Trace the pattern and cut out.

3. Open the leaf and place $2^1/2$"-3" of pipe cleaner on one end of the leaf.

4. Fold the leaf lengthwise and staple pipe cleaner; open leaf.

5. Add leaves to the banana stalk and place in the habitat.

Place on fold.

16

Tropical Rain Forest Habitat

Banana Stalk

Suggested Materials: yellow construction paper for bananas, yellow or manila construction paper or poster board for flower and stem, scissors, glue, crayons

Directions

1. Trace the bananas and cut out.

2. Trace the flower and stem and cut out. Color the flower.

3. Put the stalk together by gluing the stem, flower and bananas to the stalk base as shown.

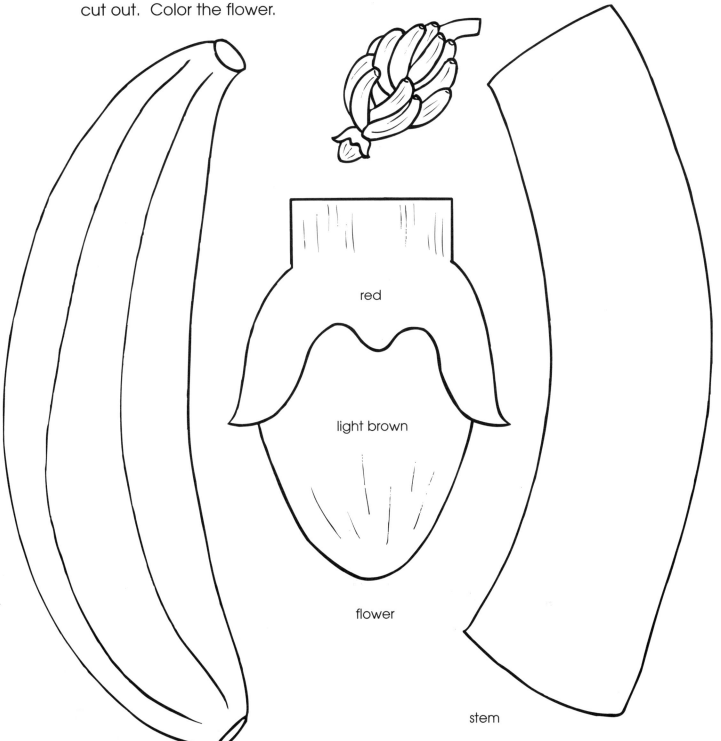

red

light brown

flower

stem

Setting the Scene
The Environment

Draw a line from the plant to its habitat.

Name _____

Trace on the dotted lines below.

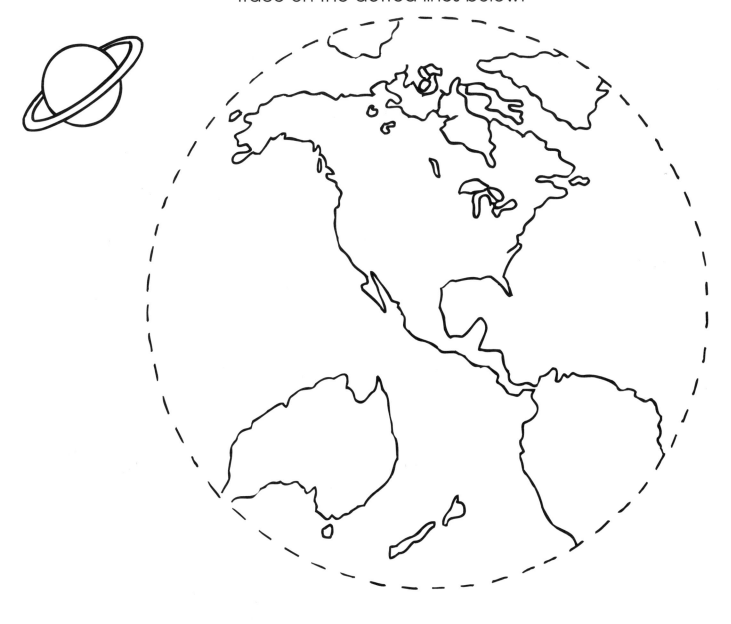

Setting the Scene
The Environment

Circle the things a habitat must have.

Setting the Scene
The Environment

Habitat Collage Mail

In a large manila envelope addressed to the class, place different sized pictures of various habitats cut from magazines, an 8¹/₂" x 11" sheet of construction paper for each child and the following letter.

Dear Science Students,

I hear you are learning about the environment. In this envelope you will find many pictures of different habitats. Choose some of the pictures and paste them on your paper to make a Habitat Collage.

Can you cover the whole paper? Where will you put your picture when it's finished? Will you be learning about the animals who live in these places?

Your friend and colleague,

Professor A. T. Mosphere

Professor A.T. Mosphere
Pro Tech University
Green City, USA

Habitat Quiz

Address an envelope for each child containing the following letter.

Dear _____,

Did you have fun making your habitat collage? Answer these questions by putting a circle around the right pictures and send the letter back to me. When I hear from you, I will send you a surprise from my laboratory.

1. What kind of habitat do you live in? _____

2. Have you ever visited any of these habitats? Yes _____ No _____

3. What do we all need to live and grow?

Your friend and colleague,

Professor A.T. Mosphere

Professor A.T. Mosphere
Pro Tech University
Green City, USA

The Environment

Hydroponic Garden Mail

Address a small box for each child containing part of a sponge; a plastic lid to hold the sponge; grass, bird or alfalfa seeds in a zip-type bag and a copy of this letter.

Dear _____,

You did a great job on your Habitat Quiz! Thank you for sending your letter back to me. I can tell you are learning a lot about the environment.

The surprise I promised you is a science experiment. If you are a scientist, you ask questions and do experiments to find the answers. Here is a question for you. Will seeds grow without dirt? Experiment and find out.

1. Wet sponge and place in lid.

2. Sprinkle seeds on sponge.

3. Place in the light but not in direct sunlight.

4. Keep sponge wet.

5. Check every day.

Did the seeds grow without dirt?

Good work, scientist!

Your friend and colleague,

Professor A.T. Mosphere

Professor A.T. Mosphere
Pro Tech University
Green City, USA

Snow-Capped Mountain

- 4 c. chocolate ice cream (mountains)
- whipped cream in can (snow)
- green sugar crystals or sprinkles (greenery)
- blue sugar crystals or sprinkles (water)
- funnels or cone-shaped paper cups

Place ice cream in paper cups and invert on plates. Squeeze on snow and sprinkle on greenery and water. Serves 4.

Ocean in a Glass

- 1 pkg. (4 serving size) flavored blue or green gelatin
- $3/4$ c. boiling water
- $1/2$ c. cold water
- ice cubes
- gummy fish

Dissolve gelatin in boiling water. Combine cold water and ice cubes to make $1 1/4$ cups. Add to gelatin and stir until slightly thickened. Remove unmelted ice. (If too thin, refrigerate until slightly thickened.) Pour into clean plastic glasses and add gummy fish. Refrigerate until set (about one hour). Serves 4.

Dessert Desert

- 3 c. cooked rice (sand)
- $1/2$ c. raisins or apricots (rocks)
- $2 1/2$ c. milk
- $1/2$ c. honey
- 2 T. butter
- 1 tsp. grated lemon peel
- 1 T. lemon juice

Combine first five ingredients in saucepan. Stir in lemon peel and juice. Bring to a boil and cook, uncovered, over low heat, stirring occasionally, for 15 minutes. Serves 6.

Prairie Picture

- 1 box alfalfa sprouts (grassland)
- 6 slices orange (sun)
- 3 cheese slices (sun rays)
- ranch dressing (cloud)
- small can corn (wildflowers)

Arrange grassland at bottom of each plate. Sprinkle with wildflowers. Place sun with rays above grassland along with cloud dressing. Serves 6.

The Animals

Discussion

Show the children pictures of different kinds of animals including endangered species. Sort the animals into classifications, such as: 1) birds, mammals, reptiles, fish and insects. 2) animals that live in the forest, prairie, Arctic and other habitats. 3) air, water and land animals. 4) animals who are pets, live on a farm and in the wild. This activity will help the children to look at animals in different ways. For example, birds may live in various habitats; they may be air, water and/or land animals; and they may live on a farm, as a pet or in the wild.

Encourage further discussion using key words for guidance. Emphasize the difference between, and the importance of, both meat-eaters and plant-eaters in the balance of nature. Children need to understand that, although the hunters in the animal kingdom (meat-eaters) may be dangerous, that does not make them "mean" or "bad." This understanding will encourage an appreciation and respect for all species.

Key Words

- **meat-eaters:** Animals that often have paws with sharp claws and sharp teeth which are used to tear and chew meat.

- **plant-eaters:** Animals that have feet with toes or hooves and blunt or flat teeth used to chew plants.

- **camouflage:** One of nature's ways to keep animals safe. Some look just like the neighborhood they live in. For example, an alligator looks like a log floating in the water, a tiger's stripes mix in with the grassy plain he lives in, a chameleon can change colors to suit his background and even a person (like a soldier) may wear a camouflage uniform so he is not easily seen.

- **tracks:** The footprints or body prints that an animal leaves in dirt, sand or snow. These prints help us to learn more about the animals and their habitats.

Key Words

- **balance of nature:** All living things depend on each other and on the conditions found in their environment (e.g., food supply, climate). One of the most important aspects of the balance of nature is the food web.

- **food web:** All living things need energy. We get energy from food. Plants use sunlight to make their own food from air, water and soil. Plants are food for plant-eaters and plant-eaters are food for meat-eaters. For example, earthworms eat decaying plant matter, and robins eat earthworms. However, it is not that simple. Both the worms and the birds fertilize the soil for the plants with their droppings and other animals (small bugs) live on the birds and eat bits of their old feathers. Discuss with the children what would happen if one of the strands of the web disappears. In that discussion, emphasize the importance of the smallest and the "lowliest" strand in the web. For example, the earthworm may be responsible for most of the topsoil in the world. (See Darwin's writings.)

- **adaptation:** (how living things change) As the Earth changes over time, animals and plants adapt to fit into their altered environment. In America and England there is a species of white moth that lives on trees with white bark. As industries grew and the air became darkened from pollution, the barks of the trees became black. The moths changed to a black color so that their camouflage would be kept intact. When the air was cleaned up, the bark of the trees became white again and so did the moths.

- **extinct:** Particular groups of animals or plants that are no longer living—that have died out because they have no food or their habitat has disappeared (e.g., dinosaurs).

- **endangered species:** Particular groups of animals and plants that are in danger of becoming extinct (e.g., some wolves, whales, bears, tigers, turtles, eagles, rain forest trees).

The Animals

Crafts

- Make a Monkey, Snake and Toucan, pages 29-32.

- Make a Track Book, page 33.

- Make Desert Creatures, page 43.

Enrichment/Language Activities

Science Lab/Study Center
(additions for existing center)

Suggested Materials

shoe box lined with aluminum foil
dirt
potato
magnifying glass
cut-out pictures of animals found in
  mountains and valleys
animal coloring books
paper
crayons
stapler

Resource Materials

- Magazines such as *National Geographic, Ranger Rick* and *Smithsonian.* Books from the library on animals including endangered species.

Suggested Activities & Experiments for Children

1. Children select cut-out pictures of the animals that live in mountain and valley habitats. Staple or tack these pictures on the Mountain bulletin board. Take into consideration the relative sizes of the animals.

2. Make a habitat for sow bugs by covering the lined bottom of the shoe box with 1"-1¹/₂" of moist dirt, a small rock, a few twigs and leaves and a potato with the bottom cut off. Children collect sow bugs and add them to the habitat. Punch air holes in the lid and cover the box. Children may remove the lid to observe the sow bugs in their habitat and note any changes that take place over time.

3. Collect evidence of animal presence such as feathers, shells, wool, abandoned nests and partially eaten leaves and study them with a magnifying glass.

4. Using the resource materials, look at pictures of animals. Encourage the children to really look at the pictures and talk about what they see (the animals, their activities, habitats, camouflage, etc.).

5. Draw and/or color pictures of animals, their homes, (e.g., nests, webs, holes, caves) their eggs, live young, etc.

Booklet

•See page 7 for general directions and pages 44-46 for specific "Introducing the Characters" worksheets.

Mail Call

•See page 6 for general directions and pages 47-49 for specific "Introducing the Characters" mail.

Pretend Time

•See page 50 for a Habitat Adventure.

Motor Time

•See pages 50 and 51 for Animal Tag, Animal Hide-and-Seek and an Animal Parade.

Show Time

•See page 51 for Pet Store, Zoo and Farm centers.

Snack Time

•See page 52 for recipes.

The Animals

Monkey

Suggested Materials: light brown, dark brown or dark orange construction paper, scissors, two brads per monkey, glue, black crayon or markers

Children choose the color of monkey they would like to make and do as much of the following as their ability allows:

Directions

1. Trace and then cut out the patterns (pages 30-31) for the monkey's head, body, tail, two legs and two arms.

2. Trace the facial features with crayon or marker and glue the head to the body.

3. Connect the body parts with brads at the Xs. Put the monkeys in the rain forest habitat on tree limbs.

Rain Forest Snakes

Suggested Materials: varied colors of construction paper, scissors, crayons

Children do as much of the following as their ability allows:

Directions

1. Using a copying machine, run off the snake pattern on construction paper (page 31).

2. Draw patterns of choice on snake bodies. △○∨∧∧∧

3. Cut out the snakes and hang from limbs or vines in the rain forest habitat.

Toucan

Suggested Materials: black, orange, green, yellow, blue and red construction paper, toucan patterns (page 32), scissors, glue or paste, string, hole punch, crayons

Children choose the colors for the wing, tail and beak of the toucan and do as much of the following as their ability allows:

Directions

1. Trace the body pattern on black construction paper with yellow or white crayon and cut out.

2. Trace the wing, tail and beak patterns on colored construction paper and cut out.

3. Glue or paste the above parts on both sides of the toucan and draw the eyes with crayon. Punch a hole in the top of the head, thread the string through the hole and hang the toucans from the ceiling in the rain forest habitat.

Monkey Patterns

tail

arm (Cut two.)

leg (Cut two.)

30

Monkey Patterns continued

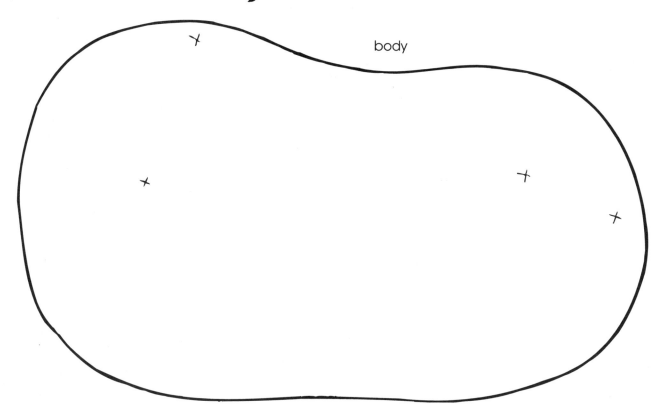

body

Snake Pattern

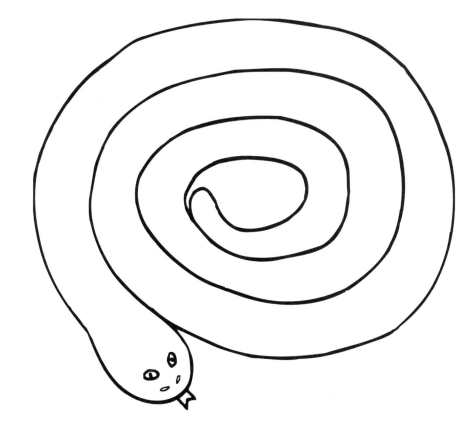

Toucan Patterns

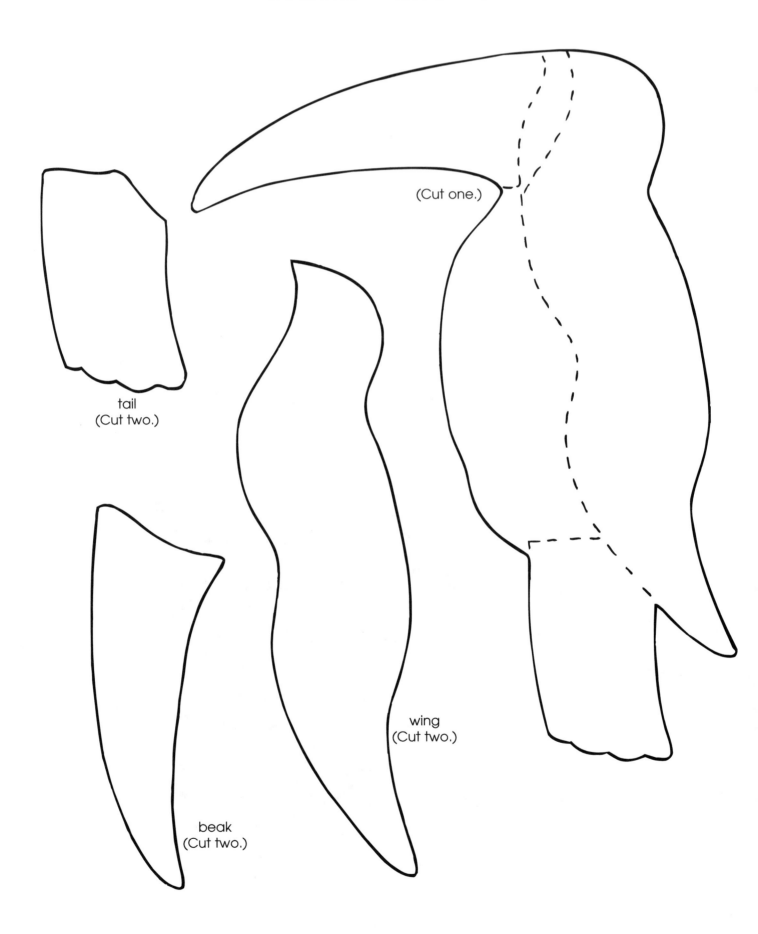

(Cut one.)

tail
(Cut two.)

beak
(Cut two.)

wing
(Cut two.)

TLC10386 Copyright © Teaching & Learning Company, Carthage, IL 62321-0010

The Animals

Make a Track Book

Suggested Materials: 9 8$\frac{1}{2}$" x 5$\frac{1}{2}$" sheets of white paper for each child, crayons, two sheets of 10" x 16" construction paper or wallpaper for cover, paint, towels, pan of warm water, stapler, pictures or stickers of animals, glue or paste, photograph of each child

Children do as much of the following as their ability allows:

Directions

1. Copy a set of animals and tracks (pages 34-42) on 8$\frac{1}{2}$" x 5$\frac{1}{2}$" white paper for each child.

2. Begin the study of tracks by hunting for snail, earthworm, bird, cat, dog and other signs of tracks.

3. Discuss the differences and similarities between various tracks (i.e., paws, hooves, body, toes, feet).

4. Children take off their shoes and socks, step into a pan of warm water and walk on the sidewalk to see the tracks they make with their feet.

5. Children then step into a shallow pan lightly coated with paint and print their tracks on a sheet of paper and title it *Me and My Tracks*.

6. Wash their feet in a pan of warm water and dry off with a towel.

7. Cut track pages apart along dotted lines. Using a stapler, assemble the book with the animal pages on top and the tracks that match at the bottom. End with the page showing the child's tracks on top and a photograph of him or her on the bottom.

8. Decorate the cover if desired with stickers or pictures of animals.

9. Children will have fun flipping pages and matching the animals to their tracks or making silly matches.

Grizzly Bear

Turtle

Deer

Sandpiper

Red Wolf

Mountain Lion

Mountain Goat

Otter

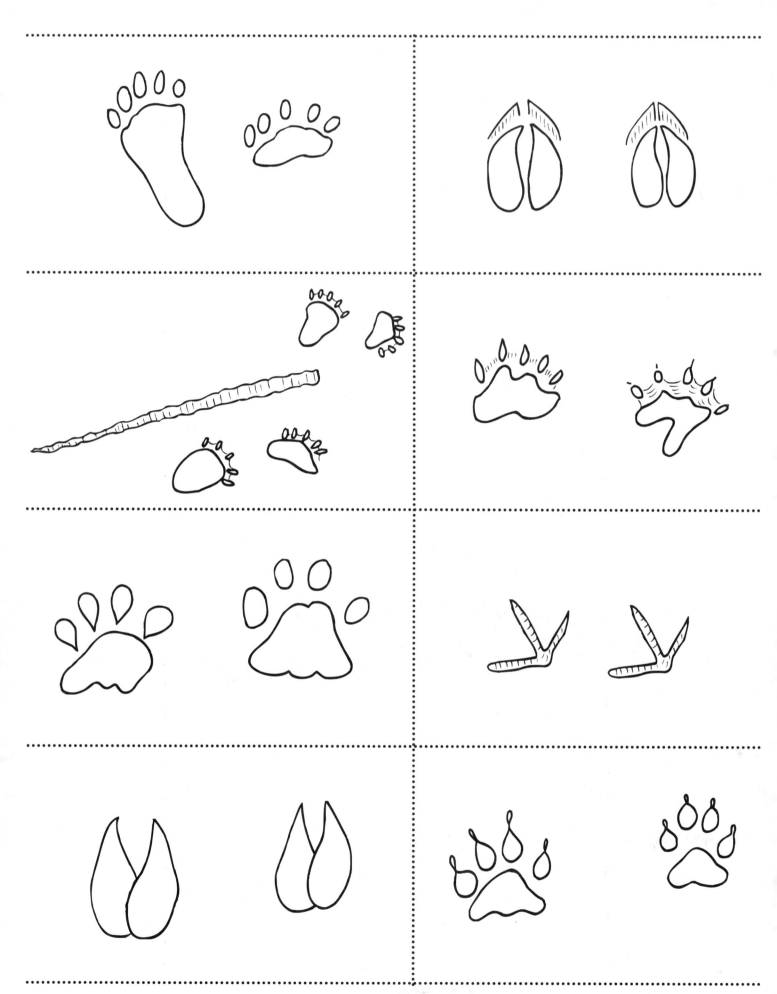

The Animals

Make Desert Creatures

Turtle

Suggested Materials: half a walnut shell, gold construction paper, pen, scissors, glue

Children do as much of the following as their ability allows:

Directions

1. Trace and cut out the turtle body on construction paper.

2. Draw the eyes on the turtle head with pen.

3. Glue the walnut shell half on the body for the shell. Place in the desert habitat.

Snake

Suggested Materials: modeling clay, either glue thinned with water or clear spray

Children do as much of the following as their ability allows:

Directions

1. Work a small amount of clay with hands to form a firm ball.

2. Roll into a rope to form the snake body.

3. Coil or position the snake to crawl, set aside to dry completely.

4. Paint with the mixture of glue and water or spray with clear spray. Place in desert habitat.

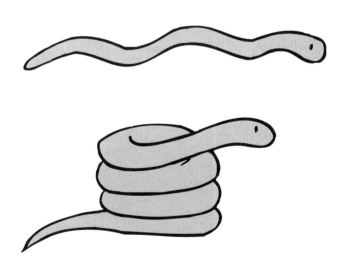

Introducing the Characters
The Animals

Draw a line from the animal to its track.

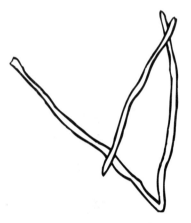

Name _____

Introducing the Characters
The Animals

Cross out the things that do not belong in the food web. Color the picture.

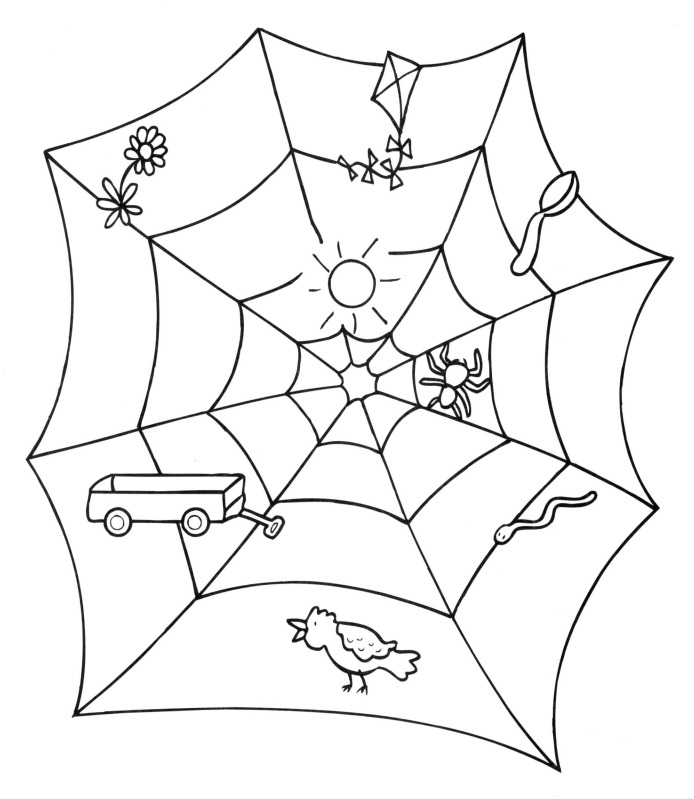

Introducing the Characters
The Animals

Color the numbers to find the hidden (camouflaged) animal.

1 = blue   2 = green   3 = yellow   4 = brown

Pocket Panel Mail

Copy, cut out and accordion fold a habitat panel (page 48) for each child. Place the panels, some crayons and the following letter in the box or large envelope addressed to the class.

Dear Science Students,

I'm sending you some of my handy dandy habitat pocket panels and colorful crayons. Can you name each of these habitats?

Use the crayons I sent you to color the panels because, in your next mail from me, I will send the animals who live in these habitats. Choose colors that will make these animals feel right at home.

Your friend and colleague,

Professor A.T. Mosphere

Professor A.T. Mosphere
Pro Tech University
Green City, USA

Pocket Panel Mail

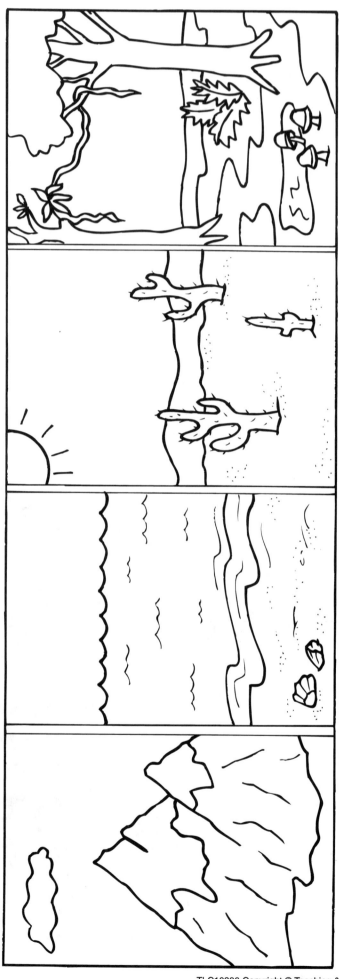

Animals for Pocket Panel Mail

Address an envelope to each child. In each envelope, include animal stickers (e.g., frogs, fish, butterflies, mammals, birds) and the following letter. Make sure that there are animal stickers for each of the accordion-folded panels.

Dear Science Student,

The animals have arrived! Now you can make your handy dandy habitat pocket panels come alive. Be careful to put each animal its own habitat. Show your pocket panels to family and friends. You'll be able to tell them a lot about the animals and their habitats.

Do you have some extra animals that have no homes? You may want to decorate your workbook cover with them.

Good work, science student!

Your friend and colleague,

Professor A.T. Mosphere

Professor A.T. Mosphere
Pro Tech University
Green City, USA

The Animals

Pretend Time

Habitat Adventure

• Encourage all the children to be creative, spontaneous and to embellish freely as they compose as much of this story as they can. Pretending and producing the animal and environmental sounds, describing the sights, pantomiming the actions and expressing feelings are important parts of this procedure. Maintain an atmosphere throughout of drama, humor or mystery as is called for by the situation. The following is a basic framework only.

Destination

• The children choose a habitat to visit, discuss what it will look like, what animals they will find there, etc.

Transportation

• Ask the children how we will get there (e.g., plane, car, ship, camel). Encourage use of imagination by asking how to start the means of transportation, what it sounds like, etc.

Choose a Job

explorer, scientist, TV newscaster, photographer, ecologist, others

The Adventure Begins

• Pretend to board, buckle up if appropriate, start, steer and stop at the chosen destination. Upon stopping, look over the habitat and check the weather (rain, thunder, wind, still). Describe the environment and its inhabitants as they are experienced. Explore, have adventures and work at various jobs before taking the trip home.

Motor Time

Animal Tag

Preparation

• Use animals stickers of plant-eating animals to make tags for half of the class.

Directions

• Distribute tags to the "plant-eaters." The other children will be "plants." The plant-eaters chase the plants until the plants are all "eaten" (tagged). The children who were plants now become "meat-eaters." The meat-eaters then chase the plant-eaters until the plant-eaters are all "eaten" (tagged).

Discussion

• Ask the children what happens when all the plants and then plant-eaters disappear. Emphasize the importance of the food web in the balance of nature. You may also wish to discuss how it feels to be chased as opposed to chasing, since each child will have the opportunity to do both.

Introducing the Characters
The Animals

Animal Hide-and-Seek

Preparation

• Use stickers or other pictures of like animals to make tags for each child. For pairs game, make twin animal tags. For group game, make tags for two categories (e.g., mammals versus reptiles, prairie versus swamp animals, flying versus water animals).

Directions

• Distribute tags. For the pairs game, one member of each pair is "it" and must find his or her twin after the others hide. For the group game, one member of each category is "it" and must find the children in his or her category after the others hide.

Animal Parade

Directions

• You will need a copy of the book *In the Forest* by Marie Hall Ets, a paper hat and a toy horn. Read *In the Forest* to the children. The children then perform the actions and make the sounds as described in the book while marching in the parade. The child leading the parade will wear the paper hat and use the toy horn. Play hide-and-seek as described in the book. The adult takes the part of the father to culminate the activity.

Show Time (pet store, zoo, farm)

Directions

• Guide the children as they create the setting for a pet store, zoo or farm and as they choose their roles as pet store workers or owners, zookeepers or farmers. Encourage them to feed the animals, clean the animal cages or other enclosures, play with the animals, exercise them, teach visitors about them and watch for signs of health problems. Some children may take the roles of families visiting the pet store, zoo or farm while others may be vets or nurses.

Preparation

• Each of these sets will require play animals, cardboard boxes, bowls for food and water, play food or play dough rolled in different shapes to represent food and a toy doctor kit. Include play money and a cash register for the pet store.

Pet Store

• Use boxes, some with cut-out bars, for cages. Shredded newspaper may be used in the bottoms of the cages.

Zoo

• Use similar cages and/or spaces to represent the animals' habitats. Green and brown butcher paper may be cut to represent grass, soil and hills. Blue butcher paper may be cut to represent water.

Farm

• Use several cardboard boxes fastened together to represent a barn and blue butcher paper cut to represent a pond.

Penguin Punch

- 2 c. low-fat milk
- 4 scoops chocolate ice cream
- 2 c. orange soda

Put half a cup each of milk and soda in four tall glasses and mix. Add one scoop of ice cream to each glass. Serves 4.

Elephant, Lion & Bear Parade

- 1 box cake mix plus ingredients noted on box
- paper baking cups
- 1 small box animal crackers
- 1 can premade frosting

Follow the instructions on the cake mix box. Spoon batter into paper baking cups and bake cupcakes. Cool and frost. Stick animal cracker on top. Before munching on the treats, line up animal cupcakes for a parade! Makes 24 cupcakes.

Ants on a Log

- 1 bunch of celery, washed and trimmed (log)
- peanut butter or cream cheese or cheese spread
- raisins (black ants)
- dried cranberries (red ants)

Cut logs in half, fill with peanut butter or cheese and dot with ants.

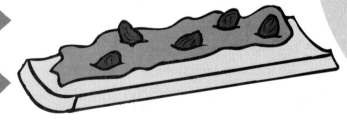

Crabby Cakes

- 1 pkg. (8 oz.) cream cheese
- 1 T. lemon juice
- 1 tsp. minced or dried onion (optional)
- 1 can (6 oz.) crab meat, drained
- 1 tsp. Worcestershire sauce
- 4 English muffins, split
- 8 slices cheese
- 2 tomatoes cut in 4 slices (optional)

Mix first five ingredients. Spread mixture on muffin halves and place one cheese slice and one tomato slice on each half. Bake at 350°F until cheese melts. Serves 8.

Pictures of the Future
Doing Our Part

Discussion

The world we live in is our home and the home of millions of different kinds of animals and plants, and we all depend on each other! Animals and plants care for us in many ways. For example, we get milk from cows; eggs from chickens; medicine, vegetables, cotton and rope from plants; fruit, wood and paper from trees; and wool from sheep. We care for plants and animals when we provide food and shelter for them, respect their habitats, etc.

If the habitats of plants and animals that live in the wild change and food and shelter are no longer available, it becomes difficult for them to continue living. Ask the children to put themselves in the places of animals and imagine how they would feel if someone stepped on their home or threw garbage around it as opposed to someone who would make a home for them or clean up all the garbage. Respecting habitats is the best way for us to protect all living things.

Here are some of the ways we can all take part in helping our plants, our animals and ourselves.

1. Recycle. (See Key Words.)

2. Do not litter. (See Key Words.)

3. Care for animals in the wild by learning about them.

4. Build simple birdhouses and put out birdseed.

5. Be responsible for the safety of animals in the wild by cutting apart plastic holders for soda cans and tying up plastic bags before putting them in the trash so birds' beaks and animals' heads don't get caught in them.

6. Stay on paths and show respect for animals' and plants' habitats or homes.

Some grownups work very hard to manage our environment in a responsible manner. They take care of our Earth by putting filters on factory chimneys, stopping chemicals from going in our water, replanting trees when they are cut down, etc.

Encourage further discussion using the key words for guidance. It is important to emphasize the concepts rather than the terminology in the discussion.

Doing Our Part

Key Words

- **ecology:** The study of the relationship between plants, animals and humans, including their habitats.

- **littering:** Throwing trash carelessly outdoors instead of putting it in trash cans. Litter can cause pollution.

- **pollution:** The air, water (oceans, rivers, lakes, etc.) and land become unclean and can damage plants, wildlife and all living things on Earth. Pollution can cause global warming.

- **global warming:** The very slow warming of the air or atmosphere around the Earth. Too much warming may be bad for crops, water supplies and wildlife.

- **recycling:** Taking things you no longer use or would throw away and putting them to a new use. For example:

  1. Give away toys and clothes no longer needed.

  2. Put empty cans, jars, plastic and newspapers in recycling bins so that factories can make new cans, jars, etc., out of them.

  3. Compost vegetable scraps, grass clippings, etc., to use as fertilizer.

Crafts

- Nesting Material Depot, page 56.

- Fly-In Diner, page 56.

- Four recycling crafts from "Suggested Craft & Recycling Activities," page 55.

Enrichment/Language Activities

Science Lab/Study Center
(additions for existing center)

Suggested Materials

juice cans; small boxes; lids; Styrofoam™ pieces; plastic forks, spoons, etc.; broken toy or clock pieces, etc.; various colors of paint; glue; old crayons; old newspapers; papier-mâché mix or flour and water; old magazines

Resource Materials

- Magazines such as *National Geographic*, *Ranger Rick* and *Smithsonian*. Books from the library on recycling, ecology, etc.

For more information, contact local or global organizations such as:

- Conservation International
  1015 18th St., NW, Suite 1000
  Washington, D.C. 20036

- National Audubon Society
  950 Third Ave.
  New York, NY 10022

- The Nature Conservancy
  1815 North Lynn St.
  Arlington, VA 22209

- Rainforest Action Network
  301 Broadway, Suite A
  San Francisco, CA 94133

- Sierra Club
  730 Polk St.
  San Francisco, CA 94109

- World Wildlife Fund
  1250 24th St., NW
  Washington, D.C. 20037

Pictures of the Future
Doing Our Part

Suggested Craft & Recycling Activities

(Making a Silk Purse out of a Sow's Ear)

1. Children look through old magazines, select and cut out pictures of man-made items (e.g., houses, cars, streets) to add to the Mountain bulletin board. Reinforce the importance of responsible use of our resources and protection of all habitats as you discuss the impact of adding these man-made items.

2. Provide a collection box for children to deposit materials listed on page 54.

3. Provide cardboard bases and allow children to glue on collected items to create a Thing-a-Ma-Jig or suggest possibilities such as a city, a building, a robot, a spaceship, strange creatures, etc.

4. Make sand candles out of crayon pieces (page 57).

5. Make rainbow crayons out of crayon pieces (page 57).

6. Make papier-mâché sculptures out of old newspapers and papier-mâché mix or newspaper strips dipped in flour and water.

7. Make mobiles or sculptures out of broken toys, clocks, etc.

8. Make recycled stationery (page 58).

Booklet

•See page 7 for general directions and pages 59-61 for specific "Pictures of the Future" worksheets.

Mail Call

•See page 6 for general directions and page 62 for specific "Pictures of the Future" mail.

Snack Time

•See page 63 for recipes.

Pictures of the Future
Doing Our Part

Nesting Material Depot (best in early spring)

Suggested Materials: half-gallon milk carton or container; scissors; hole punch; wire or string; nesting materials: small bits of yarn, hair, grasses, cotton, twigs, etc.

Children do as much of the following as their ability allows:

Directions

1. Cut the milk carton in half and throw away the top. Wash the bottom half with soap and warm water and let dry.

2. Punch a hole in each side of the carton or container (close to the top edge) and put about seven or eight holes in the bottom for drainage, in case of rain.

3. Thread a piece of wire or string through the holes in the sides and knot the ends.

4. Fill with nesting materials and hang in a protected spot such as a porch or patio.

Fly-In Diner

Suggested Materials: medium-sized pinecones, string, peanut butter, birdseed, waxed paper, plastic knife for each child

Children do as much of the following as their ability allows:

Directions

1. Lay a pinecone on a piece of waxed paper and tie a piece of string around it tightly near the top.

2. With a plastic knife, spread the peanut butter over the pinecone.

3. Sprinkle birdseed on the buttered pinecone. Then roll the pinecone to press in the seed.

4. Hang pinecone in a tree and watch the birds visit their fly-in diner.

Doing Our Part

Sand Candles

Suggested Materials: large box of wet sand; crayon pieces; paraffin; small, empty coffee cans; pan of water; candle wicks; small dowels, sticks or pencils; burner

Children do as much of the following as their ability allows:

Directions

1. Wash and dry the coffee cans. Bend the rim of the can to form a pour spout.

2. Choose a crayon color, remove all of the paper and place a few crayons in the coffee can along with a few pieces of paraffin.

3. Place the coffee can in a pan of water and heat it on low until the crayons and paraffin are melted.

4. While the wax is melting, use your hands and fingers to create the candle forms in the box of wet sand.

5. Pour the melted wax into the candle form. After tying the wick to a small dowel, lower the wick into the candle center and rest the dowel on top of the sand until the candle is hard and the sand is dry.

6. Dig up the candle and carefully brush off the loose sand.

Rainbow Crayons

Suggested Materials: small ($1/4$"-$1/2$") pieces of different colored crayons (papers removed), muffin tins, paper baking cups, oven

Children do as much of the following as their ability allows:

Directions

1. Put the paper baking cups into muffin tins and fill them half full with crayon pieces.

2. Bake at 400°F until the crayons *begin* to melt (about five minutes).

3. Remove the muffin tins from the oven and cool.

4. Peel the paper baking cups from the rainbow crayons.

Doing Our Part

Recycled Stationery

Suggested Materials: any used paper such as newspapers, colored paper, writing paper; liquid starch; optional fun stuff (flowers, grass, small bits of leaves, glitter, small threads, confetti); blender; water; 5" x 8" framed window screen; plastic tub for screen to lie flat in; smooth towels or pieces of felt; sponge; spatula

Children do as much of the following as their ability allows:

Directions

1. Tear or cut up the paper into small pieces (approximately 1").

2. Place the paper pieces in the blender using three parts water to one part paper and let stand five to 10 minutes.

3. Cover and blend at medium speed until the pulp has the consistency of thick soup.

4. Pour the pulp into a plastic tub and add a few ounces of liquid starch for body and the fun ingredients if desired. Mix thoroughly with a spatula.

5. Slide the framed screen into the tub and under the paper pulp and move the screen back and forth until it is completely covered with pulp.

6. Lift the screen out and let it drain until most of the water has drained off. Press on the pulp gently with your hand to remove more moisture.

7. Place a clean dish towel or blotter paper on a flat surface and turn the screen paper-side down on the towel or paper.

8. Lift the screen carefully, leaving the paper mat behind. Let it dry at least 12 hours.

9. Loosen from the blotting paper and gently peel it off. Let it dry overnight.

Caution!

DO NOT pour the leftover pulp down the drain! Throw it out or freeze it for future paper-making projects.

Name _____

Pictures of the Future
Doing Our Part

Draw a line to show where each comes from.

Name _____

Pictures of the Future
Doing Our Part

Color only the pictures that show the children being responsible.

Name _____

Pictures of the Future
Doing Our Part

Circle all the litter. Then color the pictures.

Recipes "For the Birds . . . " Mail

Copy the recipe book page for each child and make into a booklet.
Place the booklets in a large envelope along with one copy of the following letter.
Address the envelope to the class.

Dear Science Students,

I heard you are helping our birds by opening a Nesting Material Depot and a Fly-In Diner.

I've got a great collection of bird recipes, and I thought you would like to have some to cook up and serve our feathered friends. Bon Appetit!

Your friend,

Professor A.T. Mosphere

Professor A.T. Mosphere
Pro Tech University
Green City, USA

Pictures of the Future
Doing Our Part

For the Birds . . .

Bird Buffet on a String

- cheese cubes
- peanuts in the shell
- popcorn
- raisins
- dried fruit
- doughnuts

String tidbits and hang on trees and bushes.

Bluebird Brownies

- 1 c. sugar
- 1 c. raisins
- 1/2 c. shortening
- 1/2 c. water
- 2 c. flour
- 1/2 tsp. baking powder
- 1/2 tsp. baking soda
- 1/3 c. nutmeats

Boil sugar, raisins, shortening and water for 5 minutes. Add to dry ingredients and mix. Add nutmeats and pour into a well-greased 8" x 8" pan. Bake 20-25 minutes at 350°F. Cool and break into small pieces. Serve in a pie plate placed on the ground.

Sparrow Salad

- 1 1/2 c. wild birdseed
- 1 c. crushed graham crackers
- 1 c. bread crumbs
- 1/2 tsp. sand

Mix, roll in peanut butter and serve in the Fly-In Diner.

Dove Dumplings

- cracked corn
- peanuts
- kitchen scraps (doughnuts, cookies, pie crust)
- crushed dog biscuits
- sunflower seeds

Mix any amount of the above with 2"-3" of sand. Serve on a pie plate placed on the ground.

For the Kids . . .

Swamp Monster Snail Stew

(Read *Swamp Monsters* **by Mary Blount Christian.)**

- 1 lb. pasta shells (snails)
- 1 jar spaghetti sauce
- Parmesan cheese

Place shells in a large pot of boiling water. Simmer until soft. Drain and add heated spaghetti sauce. Sprinkle with Parmesan cheese to taste. Makes 6-8 generous servings.

All Join Hands

- 2 1/2 c. regular or whole wheat flour
- 1/2 tsp. baking soda
- 1 tsp. cinnamon
- 3/4 c. brown sugar
- 1 1/2 c. chocolate chips
- 1 beaten egg
- 1 tsp. vanilla extract
- 1 c. margarine
- 1/4 c. coconut (optional)

Mix margarine and sugar until well blended. Add vanilla and egg and mix well. Add flour, baking soda and cinnamon and mix well. Add the chips and coconut. (Save some chips for eyes, etc.) Create one child by putting a tablespoon of cookie dough on a greased cookie sheet for the body and a teaspoon of dough for the head, each arm and each leg. Put the arm of each child close to the arm of the next child so they appear to be holding hands. Flatten each mound with your fingers. (Wet fingers will stick less to the dough.) Use extra chocolate chips for the eyes, mouth and buttons down the front. Bake 12-15 minutes at 350°F. Makes 8 large cookies.

Congratulations!

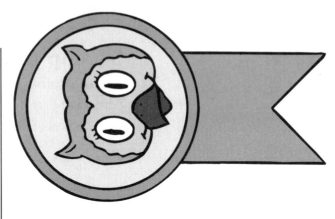

Name

You have discovered how you can
play your part in caring for
our home in space.
By recycling and respecting
habitats
you are making a difference!

Congratulations!

Your friend and colleague,

Professor A.T. Mosphere

Date

64